Know All Things To Be Like This

by

M. C. Rush

First Edition: 2020
Rs. 200/-

Cyberwit.net
HIG 45 Kaushambi Kunj, Kalindipuram
Allahabad - 211011 (U.P.) India
http://www.cyberwit.net
Tel: +(91) 9415091004 +(91) (532) 2552257
E-mail: info@cyberwit.net

Printed at Repro India Limited.

Acknowledgments

I would like to thank the editors of the following journals and websites for first publishing some of the poems collected here.

Bill Knott's Atheist Poetry Anthology Blog: "Kenosis: The Heaven of Exemption"

The Istanbul Review: "Inanition," "Maerchenkoenig ('Fairy-tale King')"

Literary House: "Drought"

Scholars & Rogues: "The Anthropocene Scene," "Angel Lust"

Taj Mahal Review: "Resistance"

Two Thirds North: "Synaptic Mechanisms for Plasticity in the Neocortex"

A teacher of poetry once insisted
that I could not make poems with words
like "pernicious reconnaissance"—

my entire career,
built on the belief
that he had no ear.

Contents

Drought

Trickling through spavined tracks,
contracted ravines eroded less rigid each day,
narrowing channels muddier, less bloody,
evincing less flex, less play, collapsed;
accustomed thirsts, urges, left unquenched
in various zealous cells that shrink and shrivel a little,
that don't drink deep—so goes the flow:
drying membranes recoil, fold, retracting,
creasing, decreasing, no longer swelled
to the rum ruddy boundary of what *can* be
by the life liquid yet gushing from the source,
the crucial spring, but drained too much,
too often, by too many, to an insufficiency,
an iniquity, a drought; as a virga rain let
drip prematurely from the gravid cloud
falls in good faith but, unconvinced,
never reaches ground; as the Colorado
surges, of course, toward the Sea of Cortez
only to get, off course, into the crust and sink,
seep below the thirsty threshold, percolate,
and drop into a different solution,
subcutaneous, colloidal, and compromised:
a less salivary salve, failing to solve—
id est, voiding its resolve—
dissolves.

The Residuum

Most everything is forgotten.

A few things, you do remember
     dismembered like May in December
reworked & rewritten, old brands reburned, new drafts
     re-encoded, reconnected, Frankensteined
neuronal palimpsests, partially-scraped
     that confound you with familiar phantoms
     reading from fuzzy myths
          descended, distended from fact, at least
          the processed factitiousness of perception

But among the representations captured, collected, combined
     are drifts of thought-fill talus, fractional fancies
not even memories, those creative construct constellations
     but edges & corners & faces rubbed off, compost impacted
compositions collapsed into grit, detritus, loose association
     from models that eroded or exploded
     dropped clippings of cerebral clutter
          that scatter over the mind's cutting room floor
          unclaimed, unconnected, without context

And this sediment, this yester-

       dust, coats, clogs
       and quells the epi-
       phenomenal epi-
       phanies, the echoes
       we brew as identi-
          tea
scraps of entirety
     confounding specificity

Apnea

but what I want to say
is simple:
though believing it
perhaps less so:
there is no such thing
as people:
only nodes
semi-knowing
to collect and categorize:
to witness and create:
but there is no such thing
as *people*:
and I guess such units
can only function
effectively
for the hierarchy
if we misunderstand
what we do
as we do:
if we believe
that we are
as we are not:
that we are such things
as we believe:
infauxmation:
but there is no such thing
as people:
the complex
impresses:

gets most attention
and respect:
but what I want to say
so simple:
no such thing
people

Poesy : Heresy

With all them monkeys
out there on their keyboards
(anyone who takes offense
at that characterization
doesn't view monkeys
as I view monkeys,
as *monkeys* view monkeys),
fingering, fretting, dense,
it's not what gets said
anymore so much as it's
the saying itself, the creative,
reactive program, running,
spinning the variations
on everything that can be said
in (and of) mundane characters,
telling all that can be told
of the trivial, the convivial,
gossips without a fence
confessing without a booth, and
yon finicky provocations yawn:
the recombinant word rolling,
the banal and the superficial
excitations, the found, the old,
the inbred, the lazy, the hazy—
throwing it all at the wall,
where it pretty much all sticks,
a lot of alliterative, aliteral,
spaghetti lyrics and lies.

The mechanical, maniacal
inputs, all so similar
(as similar as monkeys,
car keys, piano keys,
Florida keys, Esc keys,
and look-at-mes;
as common as crazy),
gleam but seem ephemeral,
and what, what will happen
when every freaking floral
unit has been described,
with passion and relief,
like shit (but with wit!);
every freakish foible
been keenly observed,
(and thus carefully
careful lie preserved);
when every silly soul has been
dissected and corrected,
faulted, then exalted,
and all the victims' airs
have been exhaled
in chatty depositions?

With all them moneys
cashing in out there,
who listens to the
posed compositions,
the susurrant songs,
imposed in this cacophony
of whispers, anyway?
Who reads, impressed,

the random recitations
but those who wrote them,
rote them, but can't
down-our-throat them?
Who will know
when to stop the pop
presses and claim victory?

River of the Dead

It may have been like water once,
cycling through a clear sky down to dry
to be filtered by soil, pure and uncontaminated
as the expectation in the young of another day
to live in, as sun-sparkled and transparent
as the ad-man's dream in a bottled water commercial,

but no more. Now it creeps and pools
across a bed with broken banks, crumbled,
uncontained, undirected. Brown and black and rust,
this viscous channel of crud lacking a true head
and mouth still vomits up a spew of muck and trash
that somehow manages something like motion.

Without edges, without sides, everything is direction,
everything is transfer, relocation. Eddies of gross gel
gurgle and retch like profane throats choking on carcasses
of half-dissolved fish. Torn plastic bags billow in the slow
current, wrapping crusted car transmissions, propane
bottles and mangled shopping carts.

Bones bang on boulders half-submerged, carved
with gouges that rise unrinsed to reflect
the ash-tinted sun back onto the rainbow-slicked
meniscus. Old objects, and new, gash the clay
of the low bottom, releasing trapped pockets of gas
that belch and boil up into the dusty atmosphere.

And yet a few go on and wade in, like believers
braving the sacred filth of a great global Ganges
to anoint themselves with the residue, with the taint,
of old wickedness, the grime of memory,
in a reverse wash that accretes layer on layer
to the skin, to the sediment of time and sorrow.

Perpendarallel

bereft? be rift
riff on the riven
rife with riff-raff
rave, raven
the ongoing internal
cacophologue, coprologue
post-traumatic reverie
a layer of frivolity
wrapped around solemnity
over a core of glee
a crazed space
a declivity of depravity
from morbid to maudlin
dark-adapted
dysfunctional, defunct
past disaster:
eucatastrophe

Bonesong

Would you have me apologize for the stench of my corpse?
You, who required a shrine of bones?

Take mine! I offered, laughing, thinking you never would
(*she won't,* I thought—I can *remember* thinking that).
How little I knew you, how little I knew the world,
and the dance of desperate acts of the people in it,
whose hungers compel them to eat, and in eating to feed
upon the supplement, the auxiliary, the ancillary.
What will evolution produce when preference supplants necessity?

Promise is a popular word for *lie* among deconstructionists
and other autophages, and you did, you did, (*the echo
of a lie as the breath disperses* and the mouth and the ear
conspire in waiting to see if it will be accepted or challenged),
you distorted your story to grant to the villain
what the hero is denied.
*Everyone surely has that moment
when life becomes stranger than death.*

All of my miraculous treasures you took, not for yourself,
not from any desire they may have ignited in your vulpine eye,
but to keep me from using them in my corybantic quest
to enjoy the world despite the world (despite my knowing so little of it).
*Is it any wonder that we who create so many ways to live
should discover so many ways to die?*

More bones! More bones! I am not enough bones,
and they are everywhere, walking free, amenable to solicitation.
You are content that no birds sing, for you will build a million perches
in your amatory ossuary and one day they will forgive you
and land on your carnal jumble and groom their dark and oily feathers
and whistle one sour note, over and over, which you will call *music*,
and which you will promise sounds as sweet as my first (or last)
I love you.

The Tragedy of Dignity

Oh, it's dignity you want, is it?

To march upright, rigid, as you
stagger straight-legged over the edge?

Better to fall akimbo, giggling,
into the abyss!

Better to flail merrily with wanton limbs
that flop and jettison woe from their extremities!

Better to taste the meat of your own tongue
than to grind others' grist with tender teeth!

Tragedy is the comedy of cowards.

Poise is a snapshot taken out of context,
anachronistic and posed, grim, grave.

It is no accident that we are born naked and screaming.
It is no coincidence that we die a punchline to our pretense to purpose.

To Must Do

(is) this (is)
what I do
what I try to do
what I want to must do
well, what I'm doing

a provocation inoculates against forgetting

oneword
    twowords
        threewords
            four

fiction is a fixative
gluing with glory
(but who seeks glory anymore
when infamy serves as well and costs so much less?)
sticking a sequence
co-mending to re-member

donewords
    newwords
        freewords
            more

a poem, no
but a glimpse, eardropped
spattered
to be inhaled as a sparky surprise

to

                         as quietly as possible

detonate and shrapnel,
be both the fuse, the fire,
the fizzle and the moan.

I was born with strength
but all my lessons have been of weakness

I want to say do not contract,

but unregulated expansion
results in identity diffusion,

so sharpen a selfless axe
for vigilantism of the tender and exposed.

Mix a verbal bolus
for suppressed defenses.

The more people who learn your language,
the faster it will change.

Better prepare an unsociable scent against
the noxious impulse toward the censorious,

for what is more repulsive
than gratuitous fear?

Suffer decent exposure.
Legitimacy is a dependent quality.

The things we use for sacred purposes
shall ever disappoint.

The Failure of the Sun

A snake can't hand you an apple;
it can only suggest one,
extolling its manifold flavors,
flavors which it learned on
its own inquisitive tongue
from fallen fruit.

Why conflate the sincerity of the snake
with bitterness? His blood is only cold
when the sun fails to heat it.

An apple is sweeter than flesh
imprisoned in dull nakedness:

I say better the tempter
than the warden. I say
better the one who chooses
persuasion than an enforcer.

I say some apples are indeed poisoned
by malefactors, but many are delicious
and some, essential.

A Six-Day Ride

No hello.
Oh hell no.
Coyote, hyena, howler monkey, gecko.

If you must spin, go counterclockwise.
You're always fetishizing a fire
but you know ice is nice.

See, something happens at just the point
at which discussion or comprehension of distance
requires a switch from ratios of length
to quantities of time:

the neighboring community lies suddenly
a six-day ride away; your life,
digitized not in segments but in moments;
trillions of kilometers become light-years,
transitioning to an ultimate extent
in which a thing *goes on forever*.

There is no forever.

Humans are parallel
but you pretend to intersect
to disguise your spin.

Inanition

dismissive
of profound intent
discursive

desire is dominant
affection, recessive

the thing you think is thin
insensible, inaccessible
the insincere in sin

instincts pester like insects
interfering

parsing arbitrary texts
for strange change
particles, pretensions

the protest of the grotesque
against lazy expectation

to propose, to proscribe
imaginary demands
with noetic license

I earth here
but cannot home

Multicore

there's a fury in the fuse
and multicore
we should all quit the circuit

emotion-augmented psychosatyrs
conjoined by history
isolated by variant code

a coven of other-lovers
conjuring private publicity
in dramatic ceremony

a circus crisis
devoid of poise
in rhombus skew

we should be folded into tents
into texts, nomadic
not installed in walls

concatenation camouflages cause

but nothing is unnatural
nothing is outside nature

why say "unnatural"
when you mean "uncommon" or "undesirable"?

fission is so easy compared to fusion
as initiative is to conclusion

The Anthropocene Scene

Impelled toward vigor,
we're demeaned by violence,
by nihilistic philistinism,
by wishful mysticism,
by competing mythologies
of those who cooperate only to copulate,
by individuality stifled with surveillance
and the cynical fratricide of civil war.

What insufferable guests we are in the world!

Go all rococo
in your mental temple,
become unfit
for civil service.

Find wanton acquaintances
and focused friends.

Brook no interference.
Reject no assistance.

Move outweird from the center.

A taboo, once violated,
deflates like a pricked balloon.

Become a person of one,
of few, or of many.

And two to avoid:
the despotic and the neurotic.

I Said

unrepented repetitions
the unyielding yields of commerce

haunt the outskirts of rot
purportedly perpetual

syncretic thesis
synthetic accretion

semantic overlooks
in the context of cortex

oneirographers of inedia
imagined favors for the hypothetical

to dream unknowing of Abaddon
the tedious redundancy of evil among the clan

imperceptible
irrepressible
malice

"I'm fine," I said.
"I am," I said.

Excesses

So much of behavior is counterterrorism,

neglecting the maintenance of proximity in a whirlwind of dread
as forced smiles become ever more grotesque.

Give me excesses, that I might craft them into resplendent simplicity,
and time, to endure the enjoyment of radiant distress.

Intelligence, undervalued because so often superfluous
in our interpersonal relations.

And bypass the consolations of deceit,
a construct of imperfect recollection,
the confusion of limited calculation,
of approximate solution.

Dwell and dwindle in disputed territories.

So much effort exhausted to make memories,
so little time to review them.

The aging brain
stultified by saturation
is inoculated against nostalgia,
as it must be.

Advertising in the Acropolis

Ergophobic Ketman,
assassin of the irreparable,
make some deprecated samizdat—
advertising in the Acropolis—
of the casual animism
and triumphal anthropomorphism
of popular thought and expression.

Gods live enskulled
between two temples
with the collusion of subroutines,
the necessary artistry of patternworking,
the externality of assessment.

Success is no excuse.
Indulge in investment.

The American Book of the Dead

Desperate
with the piety of progress/promise/purpose
to buy love and sell hate without losing our good opinion
of ourselves, coordinating contradiction in the non-ennobling
legends of twentieth-century wars, proof that democracies
too are not immune to the temptation of empire,
we have learned Hollywood's lesson of greed and violence,
of the glorification of the trivial, of the ascendance of the confrontational
priapist, while rejecting in our knowing hearts the easy sentiment
that has nevertheless managed to devalue our commitment to love.

We have heard and obeyed the edict that we should spend
so that others might profit. But the *vox populi* foments or ferments;
incidental good doesn't excuse intent; income is only one measure
of outcome. Living in complicity in a tenement of shame, quasi-
causes partially pursued, half-followed to civic nausea, everyone
selling techniques like snake oil, we ridicule what we don't seek,
what we don't think we need.

Which side do we present to the future? Front? Back?
We *spin*, standing in place, mesmerized by the fantasies
of our distorted sense, relishing embellishment, making the
petty petitions of purgatory, situated in futility, studying myths
of lascivious kindness of a kind lost to us, to me.
How could the fraudulent produce anything *but* failure?

Of what value, *glory*, when most who have sought it
have sought it through slaughter, playing life like a videogame:
action, acquisition, as a backdrop for activities for which they

accept no responsibility, questioning even causation? Bloody
does not imply bleeding. Mythology depends upon determined
insistence that this future is worth fighting for, that future
is worth fighting against, that a future of endless fighting
is the bill accompanying every birth.

We taught nature squalor.

A utilitarian must come to love violence, for it's such an easy route
to so much, but the skin remains thin, sensitive to caricature.
All promises are provisional, for *no one knows* and *nothing cares*
and *no thought transcends*. Restraint is the hardest lesson
for the wielder of new power.

We have made the wrong assignments
and are chastised—but not chastened—
by necessity's lament. Throw out, set aside,
what we've learned about how to interact with others,
how to appease their expectations and adjust our own,
and start anew, invent unfettered relations from first principles
as though we were only newly entered into life!

I'd rather touch everything
than fill it with identity,
so now I long to go overseas
investigating the differences
between our models of the world
and the world
and use false American slang,
to mess with people,
to mess with language,
to hum human hymns
before assigning them words

free of calumnies
to reclaim inquisition
from the ideological bullies,
no more to speak as a patriot,
no more to wince at hate
or to wink at fact,
but to become only myself
adrift among strangers
establishing unusual new colonies
in my insecure homeland.

Inorganic Will, The Living Expression of

I watch the river.
The water resists my attention.

We seek coherence
through a fractured crystal.

I ate words.
Some I lost and some I keep.

(I ain't words
but I'm in deep.)

The fractal rhythms uncurtailed
are exponential.

Passion
or attention to detail?

Bees don't study pollen,
obsess over the insanity of inutility.

Memory remints nostalgia into currency,
continuity.

To err here and there
is an essential part of the algorithm.

The river teaches the effect of excess
upon the earth, and proves

we can call anything beauty.

Koro

I
yearning for
textured
text

versify
my
idlewild—

long thought to be extinct—

with aggressive recombination,
culture churn.

From rags, rage—

managerial malaise
makes didactic prophylactic,

phased phrases,
faux friends,

the logical conclusion of the
image-making instinct.

The emasculation of acceptance—
is it an acquittal or a dismissal?

Damning the Phronimos

conception is compulsion

libido domini: the lust for domination

a prohibition has more force than an exhortation—
should it?

as tyrants need the fist
a horizon fenced with flags

as neoconmen of the cognicosm
grim-jawed generals
the incorporeal corporation
havoc fanatics

enemies, all

as those who presuppose an obligation
to charm approval and remuneration
from their neighboors

as the corruption of those who are proof-proof
the startling correlation of arrogance with ignorance

conformity anthems demanding
more of the same

Naked

naked
mystery is replaced
with deceit

in the nude economy
renewal of moral restriction
a relational revolution

vis-à-*vis*

the *coitio ergo sum* of erotologists
simultaneous interpreters of sex
error on error
with no chance for correction

heat-seeking phantoms
in the limbic cacophony
of encroaching crotches'
resolute carnal purpose

those inexplicably daring ones
who allow themselves to be naughty, to be nasty,
seemingly without fear of losing themselves
in sensual anonymity

naked
discrepancies are tended
covertly

Idiosynchronicities

crazed covert cravings
for the charming and the charismatic
love among the mutations
unacknowledged symmetries
undesirable congruences
idiosynchronicities
the irising siphon
of sexual apparatus
tetris genitals
the shock of the familiar
interstitial computation
when the excessive is insufficient
what are the criteria
for determining parameters of efficiency?

Patternity Test

All human thought is hypnopompic.
Even minds Olympic
have barely woken
before they retire, broken.

Always question patternity,
probe shape, estimate extent:
content isolated from context
is a model of limited if crucial utility.

If you want to throw it out,
you have to replace it
with something better—or at least *else*—
and *nothing* doesn't work.

Unknown (or forgotten) systems seem random,
subject to a dismissive inquiry;
time is everywhen but now,
contending with immiscible identities;

but without confusion there is no nuance,
though many would make much of
a Gaussian distribution
of sounds of sincerity or sex,

would say that walking out barefooted
after hints of *baraka*,
you can examine your urges
or indulge them: rarely both.

Lotophagi

i.

spare me those who cannot fathom
a universe of perverse diversity

coalition of the profligate
in virtual fugue

who underrate the inappropriate
appropriate the overrated

ii.

synchronize your pulses
opportunities for autonomy

call and response
in finicky mimicry

appreciate the proximate
with hospital frisson

iii.

said the constant to the instant:
speed cannot conquer brevity

smudge my outer particles
irascible pendant

the spin and the bounce and the bob
and all the other stationary movements

iv.

what is the universe
that it need not consume?

Resistance

step aside they say
softly at first
and easily ignored
but then ever louder
and more persistent
they begin to *insist*
that I listen to them
but I already heard them and
they may have missed it
dismissed them and
their command
their injunction
which challenges my plan
my plan
my own damn plan
which they don't know
and did they know wouldn't
understand or approve
would definitely not love
which is to step
indeed
but forward
ever forward
never back
not aside
so the air is full of stop
and step and worse
to breathe than it used to be
and my ears are as vulnerable

to the air as my mouth
which has moved from kisses
to the making of sounds
which would benefit from
but don't need
a little of that air
stopped with the starts
of the shameless scabs
the guileless newbs gathering
preparing their desperate
stampede toward tomorrow
relentlessly oblivious
to those of us
already in the way

The Sporivores

one   What is the argument
for taking it seriously?

two   We derive, we contrive,
we're alive.

three   Effort divulges distress,
more or less.

four   I, so much to see; you,
so little to do.

five   And rarely and barely
even bother to.

six   To admit influence
is to acknowledge a splinter.

seven   I want to make a thing,
not just a think.

eight   But it's harder to get noticed
than to do things.

nine   The indifferent arbiters
don't even say stop.

ten   Humanity: the universe's only
nonsense factory.

eleven   Every word, however superfluous,
              seems necessary.

twelve   Would we agree to cease
              if our memories were more robust?

thirteen   Would a mastery of words
              require their enslavement?

fourteen   Let them eat
              each other.

fifteen   More weapons are provided
              than are needed.

Synaptic Mechanisms
for Plasticity in the Neocortex

we are the shy genitals of time
riding sly orbitals of space
making chickens pay
for ancient offense
singing apocalypso
all day long

Man vs. the Memory of Nature
(some things it's a shame to see tamed)
whithersoever unjust grotesqueries
constant unconscious allusions
to process or procedure
erupting igneous ignorance
ubiquitous as lizard
ubiquitous as bug

my survival apparatus
is burdened with a self-obstruct mechanism
credulity fatigue
involuntary commitment
to associative constructions
enacting exacting practices
bereft of benefit
in lieu of impromptu improv
in lieu of glee & dreams
of love more powerful than any
dreams of love

of the tyrannical sweetness
of the sacred maids
with ancillary sympathies
and boisterous breasts
(astrogenic duffer-fluffers
living the phallic fallacy)
who enter the caves of hermits
dungskull sugarbandits
expat from all that
(antipathy anticipated
by circumspect erections)
with bioluminescent milk
lewd elegies for gastroliths
iridescented candles
looking to trade laughter
for wisdom
intoxicated intonations
halitotic revelation
of the sacred sins
but react badly to provocation

(one sound
can trip symphony
into cacophony)

the relief of compulsion
when you ask me to calculate rudiments
to measure chance and schedule waste
with the set of things that exist solely
because I'm unaware, don't know them
to cue a cure across acres of acrimony
to resurrect ethereal relations, alien alliances
to determine if exits exist

(you would think so, but)
through the sadness of the sacrosanct
fools and follies
boozing with the muse

tapping the quantum ATM
(check the tech—is it legit?)
for speech and screams
imperfectly rational
invisible signals
constructs of text
recycled wrecks
measured by marks of seizure
abrupt corruption
against the silence

don't fuss, diabolus
dark matter is cancelled matter
harmlessly useless
an efficacy deficit
calibrating composure from chaos
crass massacres
distributed community
leveraging the competitive advantage of the necropolis
to upgrade our bodies with histrionic limbs
uploaded with recursive mnemonic emotion
to overcome the remnants of philosophical trauma

From the Start...At the End

From abrupt changes in orientation,
the synthesis of consciousness...
but how can we trust perception
without knowing the principles of selection?

Our capacities
are often established
by capricious uncertainty
in lives that fall
so short of the *all*
in all or nothing:

the serfs of science, the jesters of art,
serving the lords of irrelevance; excess
analysis, glossolalia as truth-fishing,
buccal oracles, hostage to irrationalists,
dulled by an affinity for the probable;
a brouhaha of intimate tamperings,
disturbing revelations of barbarism,
the particular abstractions of neurocrats.

Everything is there from the start
except what we bring;
everything is there at the end
except what we take away.
We don't live long enough
to earn loneliness, even in our isolation,
even with our memory ablation.

Sometimes progress means *less*,
growth, a reassessed diminution—
all straight lines lead to ruin.
The problem with our roads
is that they only link us;
even in traveling them
we only arrive at one another.

Distortion

It is, is it not,
a coincidence distortion in the plausibility plot,
this evident conspiracy to circumvent
what I want,
to linger for amusement
swiping at shadows and squares of light
cursing the replacements,
usurpers of my allotment
who want to fit in or stand out,
with suspicions of malingering among the maladroit,
ranking dangerous elements
defined by the imagination of autocrats,
driven to tedium by chatbots in cahoots,
to rest and reset,
to have unprotected thoughts,
seeking a return to the solitude of the prokaryote
from the havoc of discontent,
a dispute over loot,
what we capture for our closets,
to shatter monoculture into fecund fragments,
resentment ire-idescent,
wishing destruction or defeat,
wishing everyone dead and unable to disappoint.

You would think it was more important
that we be persuasive than right.
It's perfectly reasonable. You're not.
Our composition is antithetical to contentment.
The basis of preference is the foundation of debate.

Measurement is approximate,
not entirely accurate.
You calculate to applaud the effort but not the result,
not the product, the daily reencumberment
by inadequate protocols for simultaneous sentiment
with the frustration of the finite
or the frustration of the infinite.
You ache to concatenate some moments
to celebrate discomfort,
to fornicate to calibrate
the defunct and the distraught,
the abolition of talent,
that gap between what we can tolerate
and what we *do* tolerate.
You haven't the right.

Irreverence is irrelevant,
the application of asymptomatic sacrament
as hard as hearing your own accent,
seeing the colors of current,
knowing the manufactured magic of a door or gate,
feeling a bond both a connection and a restraint.
We have all become creatures of court,
courtiers of creation, of dissolution, of sport.
And when we get bored we can invent
a new distraction, a new torment.
We can pervert and distort
words, lives, the gestalt
that we inherit.

And worse, we can bear it.

The Game With No Rules

Why a bewildering world?

Some things are not to be solved, only experienced.
The question of what to do with this experience
must, of course, be posed and solved.

Perhaps we are the incidental shadows of something
important, iterations of significance
discovered, lost,
embraced, discarded.

I am too much with me.
And too little.

Perhaps I am what asserts privilege against equality,
difference among sameness,
blemishes emblematic of infernal vigilance.

I think enough, therefore I am
agnostic about my own existence—the accidental
onus of the natural selection of thoughts—
indulging in specious visions of spontaneous good,
the *because ofs* and *if not fors*,
the contributions and other compulsions
cannibalized for advantage
in the *no-longer* and the *not-yet*.

Desire enlivens.
Desire corrupts.
Life alters.

Issuing penultimatums.

Identifying the arbitrary
in everything.

You can belong to
or you can participate in.

For it is not reproduction
but recombination.

A commotion of nuance.

The Hedonic Treadmill, Set To Eroticism

I am so tired of sex.

The quick ubiquity, iniquity of lust, us
this commercialization of cop(-a-feel ul)ulation
in which a society soaked with stupidity, cupidity
values only lascivious liquidity
seeks to elevate and enrich a solid
ancient night rite, right
overripen a natural rhythm
by monetizing it, marketing it, capitalizing a niche
selling superficially what was better bartered true
or freely exchanged as gifts of spirit and goodwill
more valuable as a commonplace
balanced upon the naturally rocking scale
of supple supply and remanded demand
the spontaneous cry of desire, fire
between waking and sleeping
than artfully, artificially packaged and advertised
controlled and contrived
as the ultimate commodious commodity, stolid
accommodating at an ongoing favor-numbing
gavel-drumming slave auction actioning actually
between faking and weeping
nesting and infesting.

Better when it was enough to feel good
for a moment
to touch another
for a moment, like a mammal

mole estrussing
and experience a brief knowing, growing
the creature comfort of connection
without shopping, hopping around
comparing product, trading up
and selling out to profit
driving a bargain down
calculating fees, taxes, surcharge
estimating hidden costs.

Now we worship sex
with its holey blessings and arrogant steeples
messy, peccant peoples, prying and poking
pray with our attention to the bodies that move us
or reasonable treasonable facsimiles
and to worship anything one must stand apart from it
separate and fetishize it, peel and prize it:
we paint it on our walls and carpet our floors with it
we plant it in our gardens, grasp at it in our barren games, names
whisper of it in a brazen shout
worded with euphemism and entendre
everyone is coated with sex
cloaked, shoed, skirted and pantsed with sex
and seen through special sex glasses
—boobs watch boobs
asses, asses—
heard only as pre-climactic chatter
the crass pitch of sameness and nameless spatter.

Is it the loss of class boundaries
the cracked glass ceilings for feelings, dealings
that has democratized desire, breaking it,
caking it on every body, streaking, striping, stroking?

What are the rules
what is the game
when everyone's a target
everyone's taking aim?
There...
oh, who is *she?*
Is she for me? For now?

I am *so* fucking sick of sex!
Sick, sickened, eremitic
(I don't have sex
and I'm sick to death of *that*, too).

His sex, her sex, their sex, your sex
old sex, new sex, show sex, view sex
virgin sex, slut sex
we-may-be-in-a-rut sex
fake sex, good sex
bad sex, food sex
rough sex, tough sex
"making love" sex
ex sex, cybersex
don't-leave-hair-or-fiber sex
joke sex, choke sex
c'mon-just-gimme-a-poke sex
president sex, clergy sex
whenever-you-feel-the-urgy sex
porn sex, pay sex
every single day sex
friend sex, stranger sex
frisky risky danger sex
dare sex, bare sex
don't-mess-up-my-hair sex

public sex, pubic sex
twisty Rubik's cubic sex
flat-on-her-back sex
and also acrobatic sex.

But every breath is foreplay
and every heartbeat
bloodpumping arousal.

Heard in every conver(t sen)sation,
scribed in every book and song
EVERYWHERE on TV
[all entertainment   (our media
                                          a reflection of
                                          our minds
                                          writ large)
is incipient porn
and vice versa]
online, mines, on the phone
in schools, duels, at home
in labs, at jobs, on the street, heat
in shops and offices, bars and churches
board meetings, cub scout meetings
planes, trains, and autoerotomobiles
in memory, in fantasy, in dream
day and night, fever
in photographs, in the mirror
every allusion, every confusion.

And when we don't see it
desperate we look again, closer
harder, faster
disappointed we feel cheated, overheated

we scream for more
we beg for whore.

Innuendo, double in tender
constant seeking, constant negotiating, positioning
arms so, legs so, smiles so
outward appearances crafted to mask inner feelings,
peelings poisoned, sanity denied, belied
so many in search of a reason to cling, a season to sing
to others, to life—how much life can we ever live
with this *brain*, these *genes*, this *compulsion*
built in? Driven to make life
not guided to live it.

How can we know each other when we can't even see each other?
How can we see ourselves when we can't even know ourselves?
When every may is deafened under a wail of must, a shout
enunciating grunts, stuttering proto-speech, animal moan
when everything is filtered, off-kiltered and half-obscured
(this half, then that half, then the first again)
behind a lacy veil of lust—lust on the inside,
lust like a crust all over the out—
how can we ever see what's true? who?

But who can remove the veil? rip it away, say, and bail?

And who would?

The baffling scaffolding of all lesser addiction
is laid, programmed, flimflammed in sex
re-pre-production, se(e-saw con)duction
it is the ultimate bias, fornicapious
and even to imagine stepping beyond its tearrible tyranny

is to envision an egosyntonic peace, sans schlepping
a qualmless calm
the world of monkey man has never known,
never owned.

Rapt in eternal rutty-smutty puberty
surging within, cycling
as the body rots and crumples without
we will always be hungry, hun-gray
always feed unsatisfied and starve large
whether feasting or fasting, feisty
and want and need and demand
and be denied
and buy, try
consume
and sell
and buy again
sold.

You are what you think.
You are.

Reflections in a River

ripple, repeat, distort
get pulled ulterior
darkening in the first pool of shade

iterations of understanding
the influence of interference
on the surreality of the mundane

time is a river
as has been said
and said and said

mind too a river
flowing both ways
inefficiently

but sufficiently

The Mumble People

ancestor of no descendant
admire without feeling
pressure to follow
the tendencies of technology
the machine as medicine
promising promiscuity
the hypothetical hysteria
the activity, acuity
of thinkers and tinkerers
designing to fit and flatter
seeking to forge it or
force it mission critical
worshipers of nuance and
promulgators of uncertainty
entranced by entry
flirtatious flashes
saying I love you when
we mean I love it
as lusting for self
in data strata
in orchestral protest
we sink into beast
handicapped by absence
assimilation lag and
practices and privileges
go from black to blank
a solitary solidarity
confronted with comfort
the mumble people

tactful tacticians
their odious odes, rapacious rhapsodies
their shameless embarrassment
their concession to concussion
the empaths and autistics
everyone who fails
everyone who loses
the feminine famines
and untaxed tech
of pleasure savants
haunted by every beast
every plant we didn't hunt
didn't eat to implicate
the implacable cavernous
carnivores insisting on insertion
into commingled mythologies
with usurious luxuries

I want to eat
but am uncomfortable
with the loss of the eaten

Rekalkenor

a day, a world, some paper
a certain insignificance of talent
a certain intransigence of creation
reduction or enhancement
concealment or revelation
the distractions of precision and clarity
confounding cognitive cartography
with tabloid dissensus over the Mokele-mbembe's
photo pas

steady as she goes
sugarbrain
solid as she comes
the sacrificial artifice
warm, not incendiary
seeking the sublingual
cool, not chilly
of any imminent moment:
all superstition is local

teasing technicolor codpiece
toys, not tools
thwarted optimists
joy, not jewels
reverse-karma
trickling back from the future
aube glowing over
the shoulders of *los malos*
anticipating dread

Maerchenkoenig

("Fairy-tale King")

Neurotypicals, blissfoolish, enchanted by charismatic megafauna,
autodidactic dataddicts adducing dialectical dactyls
to habituate inclination into tendency,
can only digest oversimplification;

unaffiliated scholars, nerd bards of frenetic stability,
quiet chaos, calculate the density of a neuron star,
seek the strange, long for the unusual, pine for the odd,
fight fictional factions from a book of comforts.

There are those who work
to admonish the monkish
and those who would polish the dull,
deal the foolish a penalizing future.

Examine their calculations of the distance
between the vandal and the iconoclast,
the commercialization of the urge to destroy,
the pissing on idols of the cult of the anti-mainstream,

taking art apart with a postmodern primitivist's rejection of order,
lust for the moment, refusal of continuity.
Don't capitulate to regret
like the vicious little pissants.

Is it that madness comes
to all who are inadequately distracted from its approach,
or is it there, epiphenomenon of energy enmassed,
from early days of cranial condensation?

I don't know how much resistance is optional,
but I'd prefer you not interfere
with my intermittently widdershins inclinations.

Consensus 2

we eat the apple of birth
to escape the Eden of nonbeing

to compensate
for deficit

a consensus may coalesce
that says you're one thing, more or less

dogma doggerel,
folksy folderol

every medium
an oversimplification

(literalists destroy legacies,
ever have,

their definitions even more unreliable
than their assessments)

so the indecipherable
are the most miserable

like Greeks
camouflaged among hostiles

like Trojans
asking what the Helen
is going on

a truth untold
feels untrue

the intrusion of the single song
defends the muse against the bemused,
the ever-obtuse boasts of the grandiose

we can only remember what is past,
we can only hope for what is not

water, ice on the run

then
in a moment, you are turned around
reversed
reviewing

    desperate wordswirls slambamming
through culture barriers of sentiment & overfamiliarity
erected in shadow by strangerkin
in fond indifference & wicked love
    personal habits functionally fixed
a little at a time at a little brittle time
by a glue of dewdrops beading in the pores, the ponds
drying to a hidebinding residue of whatever
    happy warm & easy

ice & water & icewater   & drops
    then drips
    then streams
    then pools
   of icy water, that freeze

  ice is slow water
  water, ice on the run

slow lessslow fassster faster fast

tentativity creeps toward certainty

fluidity precipitates into solidity:

all came to pass as they said it would:

the dog died, the friend lied, the girl cheated

& the mind went slowly to sleep

& dreams of moments manufactured

of sparking sentience

& other errors of inexperience
aching

& fading

Compromise

I am waiting for nothing
to happen.
                    —Felix Pollak

Then they point a gun at your head
and make you choose: interesting or useful?

Sometimes the most important thing in your life
can't outweigh all the other important things in your life
and must be sacrificed or left unrealized.

This is disaster.
This is compromise.
This is loss.
This is life.

(but note that compromise
is not a Commandment)

Apparent strength
reveals weakness.
Nothing can survive repetition.

Helplessness is not happiness,
though it leaves you contented and constipated.
If you are going to make your life smaller,
be sure to make it truer,
or at least better.

Desire, too, is an affectation,
as is the decision to walk away from desire.

   (it will follow, relentlessly
    it will follow)

Does happiness have the right to pursue me?

I can be realistic, have been realistic,
but for now am not interested in realism.
I want to watch my mind warp reality
into patterns that I choose—or at least approve.

   (my familiars are holding me back—
    *I need a plunge into the madness of the differ*ent)

Just imagine what you can't imagine.
The plausible is not always actual,
the actual not always plausible,
though plausibility is our favorite torch
to hold before us as we blunder through darkness.

Real strength
accepts weakness.
Nothing is the least I can do.

Joy pierces a moving target.

   (as does regret,
    but less)

Confinement

we're all neighbors
all strangers

adjacent incompatible

so much alike we can't
tolerate looking at one another

incendiary expectations

magnifying tiny variations
into hatred

to shush and shame

desperate to leverage what we have
into what we want—

we *can't*, we *can't*, we *can't*!

your inhabiting your space
confines me to mine

the opalescent illusion

maybe it's all so we can learn
empathy through regret

how proud we can be of our regret!

everyone antagonizes the protagonist—
why can't there just be one of us?

or

why must we be so nearly
similar enough to merge?

malevolence is the easy way out

Something For Everyone

if memories are inauthentic,
is forgetting a pledge to truth?

ADHD—evolution's answer to
looking into the void?

we are attuned
to the illusion of significance

a dormant potency
in the frivolous and the philosophical

wired to enwonder the world
without obscuring it

logic is an historical symmetry
in a world of fractal calculation

the pantheism of neologists
listening to paleographers, profits of newledge,

mystics of culturomics
with their innovative demonyms

the lovefaking
of the rationalizers' *cri de coeur*

over insuperable microadventures
a bit too anything-goes

teratologists
self-terrorists

Capaneus
ghost-fishing
the necessity of tomorrow

My Mutinous Design

as we age, as society fractalates into complexity,
we are increasingly confronted by phantasmagoria
insisting we acknowledge it as legitimate

but the only appropriate monument
to superstition is disdain

if there were a god,
confronted with our stupidity
it could say only stupid things to us

show me a veil and I will lift it   and I will leave it
show me a knot and I will loosen it   and I will tighten it
show me a lie and I will deny it   and I will buy it
show me a shadow and I will light it   and I will hide in it

praise the time of mutant children
acknowledging the futures

gunfire
tears
gunfire

they've got to improve the news

Motley

the young on the run
on errands of error
sodden in a pit
denied hedonic values
skin self-graffitied
mostly motley
desire self-gratified
powder too damp to be lit
some sameness of summary
of summery sums
summarily summoning
someone

Angel Lust

the pedantic romantic
his somatic compunction
his chaste waste

the static charge of arousal
is just that, static,
without the impetus of action

the semiotic semi-erotics of
formative fornicative experiences
mislead without falsehood

impulse
spurious vaginal angels
petrichor to mithridate

shamanic shagman
caress a rough flesh of lump and crease

Austerity

> "Mad, but beautifully mad..."
> — Carolyn Kizer

my instinct to war against reality positions me against its defenders,
those despots of assumption about the unassimilated data
(though I judge them only deluded, not deranged, insufficiently subtle)
coercing commitments from the credulous about the desperate
cleverness of life—all the little cowards hiding behind the illusion
of specificity, tending their wounded understanding
with their *eureka!* and other ejaculations

(I will not comment on their love of shame)

maybe we're misdirected by the agendas of the mapmakers,
maybe the brink of madness is the center of sanity
maybe each generation must develop new skills of orientation
using our most sordid inquiries for disambiguation
(what would anything be without perturbation?)
calculating the amplitude of ambivalence as if
the incorporation of data leads to congruence with reality

truth reveals truth
lies reveal truth
silence reveals truth

the consensus of consciousness
the clutter of experience
the ego mess of imagination—
how they pass the time
like a biscuit to someone else

confined to the middle zone, excess reduced to essence,
we remain ignorant of extremes and therefore question
borders, edges, boundary

why begin anything when there's no time to finish it?
the world is poisoned already with beginnings

it's not that we have to traverse darkness to reach light
it's that both beckon us follow to move forward
and if we don't keep moving we die to the data-gray,
becoming choral robots
synthesizing song
like Mozart, like Bach
(but not, perhaps, like Beethoven)
from the computronium

Situational Aesthetics

revel in the revelation
of altered process
terror risen in
core rectitude
aptly synapsed
by mute mutterings
of the continuity from
sensual impulse
to weak collection
the pose of poise
a poison frozen ooze
the apogee of embolistic
comprehension
caress to possess

How Can You Expect Someone?

"Show me how you kind of pretend yourselves,"
said the epiclectic xeriad, prehensile, apprehensive.

It's a birth effect,
hosting memetic codes.

"I will share your meal,
so don't eat everything you kill."

Heliogabalus.

So many years in the desert now.
Uninterrupted conversation.
Unspoken conversion. Dry mimesis.

What we want is the unexpected,
not the unexplained; the surprise,
not the lies.

Even the evident attracts dissent,
mute attempts to communicate.
An observation of coincidence
confounds more people than a riddle.

Accommodate, don't acquiesce.
Obsession can accomplish
order and/or retention and retrieval.

Look around.
Someone in the room is dangerous.
Even if you are alone.
Especially if you are alone.

How can you expect someone
to take the time?

Kenosis: The Heaven of Exemption

You dream your Adam an amoeba
To break his eukaryotic whole
And split in two his God-made lonely soul,
To clone his greed, great cowardice,
And make another apart to blame
(For, Michelangelo notwithstanding,
Pointing the finger at God across the chaotic sky
Is less than satisfying):
Your darling Eve, a wanted wanton
At once silly and deceitful,
The easier to ridicule and despise:
The mistress of distress, the mother of all lies;

Unjustly shoved from the garden of supernatural love
(An insipid primordial paradise, where nothing changes
And choice is an uncherished illusion)
By the remote Father figure with His imperious concerns despotic,
The impossible demands, fatal reprimands,
Who trips so that they will fall—
The broken couple shatters in shame,
The apple falls close to the tree,
Their children murder and nest
Incestuously to people the deserts with sparks so demonic
They must be drowned in dark and deluge and death;
Later women and afterward men
Are damned forever for every disagreement
(Whether of diet or deportment):
Every natural thought is made impure,
Every reasonable word a blasphemy,

Every act but strict obedience
(To a silent god who doesn't speak,
Whose every command must be invented,
Interpreted again by fickle men),
Conveniently, a sin;

Never has such a fuss been made over a dead man,
Whose words, once trivially grand, were with the breath
Immediately stolen from the mouth of his corpse
By those who then inverted (and thus perverted) them—
Messianic miracle! the dead is risen! (but reduced
Via reverse transubstantiation in cruciform embrace)—
Swapping purity for power, salvation for control,
To build a Christian fecalith of fidelity
Before which all are commanded to kneel
And likewise worship death, subvert the real;
To build arrogant cathedrals with priapistic poses
Struck to impress the naïve, the poor of purse, and worse,
Those who can't much think and only feel, and seduce them
To sacrifice, to orgies of piety and prayer,
With the quick spells and misdirection of self-sainted stage magicians
Working to obscure their sacrilegious trick,
The mean motive of their mission,
Their message of nightmarish hell and eternal damnation
From which the worldly lords who lead them,
The chattering claque of clerics,
Enjoy the heaven of exemption:
Let the hungry lions eat meat while the saved sheep weep;

And preach of fear and limitation,
Lamenting man and his weak and crooked core
While embodying all the sins of their own designation
In self-fulfilling prophecy and in sermon citing litanies of

Human weakness to justify those transgressions
Rather than their secret certainty that there is
No force behind their farce
But that which they themselves provide
In servile bonds of shame, in pillories of salt,
Freeing them to feed in contrived rituals of tears:
Pagans purged,
Parishioners punished,
Peccant priests provided for,
Popes pimped like primordial pop stars
Of sick and sacred appetites,
And a hapless world of fools at fault the feast;

Embracing a pieced-together tribal bible
Boasting intolerant values of violence and vengeance
Renamed "love,"
While denying any possibility of earthly justice
For those who bleed, the blessed;
Excusing themselves from the responsibility of bequeathing it
And trading even the forlorn hope of achieving it
For impassioned promises of a postponed reckoning
And high exalt, a posthumous reward
Rendered above by another hand;
Espousing revelation by a band of men dead
Before ninety generations of our grandfathers were born,
Ninety generations over which nothing has happened,
God has not appeared except in the delusions of the mad
And the starved dreams of the needy—
Confusion: you cannot witness what you've never seen—
And most advances by man and in his society have come
Not guided by the rote rule of totalitarian religion
But despite it:

The ideal scam is one in which there is no threat
Of discovery (and therefore no accountability)
For those who perpetrate the fraud;
Fantasy ends at the body's grave,
So enshrine innocence (a pretty term for ignorance),
Encourage childish superstition, preach against what seems,
For if only the lost can be misdirected,
Only the shaken shaved and enslaved,
Then all meaningful maps must be discredited
To sell the scheme:
Faith is a feeling for the false;

All true prophets are heretics;
Exploration is inherently deviant;
The dangerous must always be damned:
Galileo & Darwin—Discovery & Dissent—
More precious than Jesus
And no less crucified
By those who knew—and cared—not what they did.
There are two types of men in the world:
Those who want to be gods
And those who don't want to be
At all.

Lunch

Luftmensch questioning the kayfabe
subject to sumptuary restriction
concatenating surreal non sequiturs

a shock to freak out your follicles
a single, a solitary, a lone
some blows are low

money-squandering
runway runaway
collating worstsellers

freedom * pleasure * purpose

if I am everything
what hegemony do I have
over my infinity of parts?

for gods and other self-appointed bullies
no dull nodule whatsonever
stymied by trivial essentials

only sometimes should we prefer
some humdrum lunch
over the frenetic kinetics of idiot poetics

The Shadowcasters

we long (why?) to approach close enough to stars
esoteric hysteria desire for terror nonsentient
sentinels' blame without fault seeking the shadowcasters
that they might chastise us with blindness

we may fail because we have
domesticated what we needed wild—
give medals to the insubordinate!

to resist is to lose—
don't resist, refuse

pursuing the sound of sound,
the color of color,
the taste of taste,
is missing the point—
diminuendo

once you've been held—
once you've been held down—

ember in amber,
remember?

entropy requires heathens in heaven—
a haven of loss as much as hell is—
none who understand would go there

what we are offered now
are opportunities to repeat our battles
unto perfection to swing
and swing again with improving aim
achieving ever-finer ratings of destruction
while holding back the final launch
that instigates the end—
soldiers are boring

we can *pretend* to sate
our hatreds in inconsequent release
though in so doing we reveal
the fuel that daily chars the walls
around our hearth, the same we rejected
when victims victorious we took the lease

what fool said hell is based on fire?
fire effects change, alters matter without restraint,
while hell is permanence
permitted no change ever—
forced to close
in the midst of opening

damnation is the judgment that you never did
what you should have done
and your chance is gone

I say error should fall away
fault without blame
where accomplishment aggregates

to heel and ankle affix thy fangs!
your bite will abide without distinction
among my incidental wounds,
decorating my stride with faithless filth,
elaborate inscription, which rises
not to vex my navigation along
the route of well-doing

the question of whether I belong
in heaven (or in hell) is moot until
I'm made to want one or the other

Imagery of the Imaginary

I imagine jasmine and honeysuckle,
but nothing grows as I want it to grow,
nothing thrives
inside
desperately seeking saccades
from moon to noon
every habit, every taboo revealed
a step toward enlightenment,
colloquial epiphanies,
asymmetrical homeostasis,
irregular coherence,
the projects of prophets
overwhelmed arsy-versy by avifauna,
exchanging bits of myself
for bits of not-myself
until I again become myself,
purpose deflected into usefulness
through a narrow gap
between expectation and denial.

How much is
yet not available?

The Noble Gesture of Assertion

All teaching is assertion or demonstration.
There is no profane mania,
so celebrate the amplitude of deviation:
identity is aptitude plus attitude,
anger at the perpendicular,
a surfeit of surface.

No one remembers the second man to bring fire
and no one remembers the first
or the talons he suffered,
though we tease a homunculus with immortality
and a lackadaisical gratitude:
betrayal is a concession that honor is a construct,
a tragedy of inconvenience.

Doubt and madness,
the yellow flame and the blue,
excite the only heat
that can melt the brittle ice of conviction.

Eyes that don't open on schedule,
that train on a partial view,
develop a perverse vision:
what you don't see becomes what you can't see.

Fools worship the light the wise use to see
and who's to say that Narcissus
bewitched by the meniscus
even *acknowledged* himself?
It takes a negative mind to malign a fascinated attention.

Without intent, no accident,
the hypertrophy of unintended consequence,
the tao of the Tao:
burn with a scream or a song,
the inspiration of computation,
the great ghee of comprehension,
the embarrassing redemption of consumption,
the predictability of arousal, of subsidence.

Tears and smiles both conferred an advantage
and so we cry and grin in mammalian huddle:
better the communal accretion of the hard coral
than the acute congregation of the soft moral.

Minutes are no more manageable, imaginable, than millennia,
but they are embraceable.

Know All Things To Be Like This

If consciousness is a lens on chaos,
an invisible fractal focus,

and yet a fixation with images imperils continuity,
every moment a transient bardo, a gap overlapped,

if things are thugs,
perpetrating violence,

diminish your grief without guilt,
release your guilt without grief.

There is an anomaly in the heart of things
and we have a gruesome duty.

I can enjoy the absence of pain without celebrating it:
the pursuit of solitude is also a catalyst of loss.

Study attachment vs. commitment,
serenity vs. apathy,

the tyranny of chemistry,
where freedom consists of exploiting the code.

If mystery itself conforms to formula,
then mastery of rules is the only escape from tedium.

How to maintain respect for the Law
when laws are lies?

Curiosity for the revelations of rediscovery
within a societal hive which has not yet begun to exhaust naivete?

Desire for the products of sacrifice,
of disincarnation?

What won't the committed
distort to their bias?

We lope in loops
with the helplessness of a corpse.

Enjoy illusions,
but don't love them.

Omnivalence

The dead have censored the past.
There's nothing more relevant than irrelevance,
rife with iconoclastic fantasies of a dangerous world
or a comprehensible one, of the interdependencies
of pursuit and escape (I would add "capture," but I'm not
sure I believe in the phenomenology of capture).

Overwhelmed at work,
hopeless at home,
bewildered in bed,
comfortable only
in front of the TV
(which asks so little of us,
accepts our strongest criticisms,
compels our worship
with reverse offerings);
emotion junkies predestined
(or merely predisposed?)
to insist on free will
(I choose to pursue the unthinkable
but not to live with it),
on the enthusiastic embrace of ugliness,
on trying to avoid the void
while communing with the ambiance of the dead,
while calculating potential outcomes;
the stubborn pilgrims on pagan footpaths
shall outlast the Christian highways,
displaying their sins in order to smuggle
their decency through society

in a country of convicted innocents
threatened with the occasional breach of security.

All saints are sinners' patrons,
(all) sacraments are sacrifices
impersonating inhuman things,
difficulties and disappointments, remorseless
lovers living with desperation's decisions
from one fuss to another, shunning
the dialogue of shunning, reprogramming
economic imperatives to isolate the contingent
of resisters (apparently I don't like being
encouraged to like things)
(why is it so important to you
that I want what I don't want,
buy what I don't need,
become what I don't like?)
while camouflaging everything
with the false glamor of obscurity
(the better part of the hidden
is merely unencountered)
flavored with a false sense of reprieve.

Sacrifice for is an improvement
upon sacrifice to (my intention is evolving),
but it's still a scarification.
Original. Of the origin.
The origin of *what*?
Skepticism and wonder.
Once nostalgia has you,
you're over. (And how
do we choose between pursuit and wait?)
Cognition is based on obsession.

Dependent upon matter and energy,
but neither. Soldier without sanction.
The one who knows everything and does nothing
(judgment is not synonymous with condemnation),
the wisest and the most culpable.
We want to give thanks for the world
and its little glories, but no one cares.
The void is the random. The candid man can
describe gratitude for random gifts.
Don't trust tomorrow's strangers
to care for our treasures.

Incorporating Accommodation
for Future Augmentation

1.0   abandon the abominatrix
      preference is not necessity

1.3   prep for urbex

2.2   confront with
      the linearity of rail
      or marital email

2.4   carry the train of the bride inside

3.1   use your peripheral intelligence agency
      to ascertain whether evil is inherent or internalized

3.8   blame gravity for the grave

3.9   go out with an interrobang

4.0   *regressus ad originem*

4.1   counter disinterest with spectacle
      with the immodesty of immolation

4.7   a bird in air
      is worth ten in hand

Banal, Brutal

people

who never feel safe enough to indulge emotion—
or never emote enough to feel safe

who confront honesty with rebuttal,
with retort

who hear only the music of the spears,
the lying lyric of fear

public pulses

dedicated to delights
motivated by frights
attracted to lights

worshipping axioms of adaptation,
sensitive to rebuke
but not to the similarity between fear and euphoria

to each his owner,
terrorized by awe,
the imposition of adulation

all forsaken by all

with or without consent,
with or without intent,
before or after we fall

into unrecovered subterranean chambers
carefully prepared long ago
yet waiting

banal brutality
brutal banality
harrowing hype

bigotry ubiquitous

in god is lust
for dust-covered erotic ivory icons
in keeping with exotic evangelism

congenital mysteries, inherently secret...
what is lost, what is *missed*
is subtlety

strategic zombification,
a revelation of insecurity
big enough for a microcosm

Homunculus Rock

Be alert to the eventual deafening
by the constant clanging
of the continuous banging
up against our limits.

If you need heroes, look no further
than all those names which didn't escape the flames.

Go sip some gossamer summer gossip, irrevocable ear vocals,
geek chic technologistas, *kiss me* signs still stuck to your backs;
ignore the monomaniacal moneychasers, superstitious schizophrenics:
the Treasuremaster is always hunted by the Trashseekers,
trudging through deteriorating clutter in toxic mud,
crippled by blisters, self-defeating defects,
acquired along our death march, an interlude of decrepitude—
try us, detritus! We'll make every kind of noise.

Roused by a scintillion impressions, similes desperate to imagine similarities,
nudged, coaxed, commanded, convinced until we accept perception,
dreaming of a world that smells of frangipangi and honeysuckle
and tastes of cayenne and habañero, clothed in cumulonimbus,
while encouraged from many sides, including the spiritual and the rational,
to wean ourselves of worldly things, to seek succor in wordy things,
or no things.

Sudden. Certain.

When the law becomes arbitrary, the lie is revealed.
Balance is always precarious. Men menace.

Every revelation, another weakness.
Our machines must increase in sophistication
until they can speak of our extinction:
our words in their cadences.

I scoff. But it's not enough.

Indulge

indulge
in all manner of

in time
intolerable

intricacies

interests and
inclinations

and if this
doesn't,
then what?

intent
is porous

Homogeneity

relinquish your unorthodox paradox reluctantly
forgiveness is a disincentive for getting it right

dogged by the superfluous
surrounded by the extraneous

we suffer a surfeit of surface
a surplus of skin

redundant accompaniment
shadows stacked to black

crowds convening and congesting
traffic routed into jams

all the silence is locked in the past
the future is noisy and irresolute

and now is tethered to an uneasy anxiety
like a balloon bobbing in a hailstorm

"soon" promises everything
that still bothers to promise

and soon means never
as it ever did

an atom matters in a molecule
but living caricatures catalyze little

when did I lose my capacity to have favorites?
I still love, but I no longer love one above another…

The Ebook of Lamentation

evolution is a concatenation of errors,
compromises

the necessity
of a few things
that can't be justified

some for the caves
some for the trees

consequences of consciousness
a recent rearrangement

imitating the sounds of the world
in abbreviated homage

I want a smooth and shiny
rapt in admiration
pulsing in place
eddying with inspirational drift
laughing
with the poems of raindrops
landing

I can't hold quiet enough
to keep the rock
from chastising me with echo

you say "a long life,"
I laugh

patina
becomes part of the pattern

Anthrotoxic

aerialists or waders,
our progenitors knew
how to move

but one can celebrate what has been gained
while still lamenting what has been lost!

billions of dead
waiting to be remembered
when there's no mechanism for memory

to be isolated from context is to be
the number of fish in the sea
in, say, 1000 C.E.?

I'm this many

where are the universal keeners
mourning every little loss?

every teardrop ever shed
encased in a bubble
(one each, not all in one)
and risen into clouds
miles thick
that would chill the Earth
and kill the dinosaurs

taut webs of meat
ruined into greatness

we hurry for reward
toward madness

Capriccio

relish the relics of growth
cast off by the stagnant
a community without continuity
collaborators in hours and words
cloud watchers
scrutinizing sanity
perilous scrutiny
as disillusioning
as entropy

release the comfortable falsehood
of the uncanny valley
populated with historical enigmas
too puzzled by people
to craft well-rounded characters

realize the goal of philosophy
is to reword old questions
in new ways such that they
are cut loose from the reward
of old answers

Flight From the Gnomes

Twilight dims the world now
and only memory flares rise to burst against the even sky,
memories like the time my cradle was robbed
by sorry gnomes with swollen noses and jutting rumps;
tumbled from the crib
I eluded their splayed paws
and rolled downhill for longer than I'd expected;
when I came to rest
I stood, mottled with dust and bruises,
and stood numb and dumb
gaping at the engulfing wilderness
wild with shrieks and cries
that echoed my personal lament;
I rolled in the mud till I was hidden;
I followed a silver stream half-choked with debris
from which I dared not drink
to a happy spring that first mystified
then angered me;
up through a million villainous leaves
I saw the gray sole of space
fill with clouds that gathered and threatened,
thickening the atmosphere with tension
but offering no release;
now and then a beam of light lit wonders in my eye
and windows in that sky,
and fires in my breast,
but fuel was scarce
and they smoldered and gutted
to little piles of golden ash;

and darkness came to the day
long before night,
and all that I can recall
is being lost
without a map or a companion,
no guide at all,
and all that I have been
is being lost
in this hidden glade,
this shadowy grotto
where blind fish whistle like the stars
and I am safe from lumpy gnomes
with watery eyes
and alien concerns.

confusing want with need
we feed

when we idealize similarity, simplicity
and demonize difference, complexity
when we think we can be safe
or need comfort
when we elevate the ignorant
or cast down the knowledgeable
when we ignore others' agendas
or deny our desires
when we accept others' assessments of us
and forget our own idea of who we are
when we accept without challenge
when we act without thought
when we believe
when we give in to manipulation
implement policy based on fear
when we buy what should be free
when we cultivate ingratitude
with more enthusiasm than food

the Earth is slow to respond to our criticisms
after millions of years of being good enough

The Ironic Chronicles

A retreat from certainty doesn't
have to be an advance on chaos
if one knows where to bivouac,
taking delight directly in things, the things
that people have imagined and made real,
or in devising ways to separate from them,
contravening the conventions of conversation,
the revelatory perversion of irony persecuting
accident mistaken for inevitability, happiest
swimming and drowning in connotation
when we don't appreciate its pathology, our correlates
too proximal (the most artificial thing is a hierarchy),
adversarial or combinatorial, oversight or observation
reverse-engineering reality, relationships,
to list implicit assumptions with erroneous honesty
striving for accuracy while incorporating renunciation
of some of the extraneous (but what is necessary?),
a generosity of interpretation obsessed with the unperceived,
the sur-unreal, the trite parameters of invention,
innumerable opportunities presuming to exhume the future,
the hidden, the hideous, according to the evitable criteria,
the pose of expertise as a corrective to excess,
the negotiation of disadvantage, of what is said, what
doesn't register, what isn't remembered, what is
misremembered (remembering feels a little like learning,
like a little learning), pronouns getting ever vaguer,
the diluted power of a renaming yet makes, yet erodes,
new shapes of meaning, putative computations, the artifact
of art-in-fiction, admiring the self-defined, the self-defiled

(phenomenon or specimen?) over those practicing paleologism
to corrupt the vulgar to nicety, to behavior unbecoming to the robust
but a lot less fuss.

There are interesting things that no one has time to notice
evaluating category errors: the subtlety of some lessons,
minority interpretations, the part of assessment that isn't calculation,
essential waste, strangled and shoved into categories too narrow,
wrapped and bound by labels too broad, trivia-addled, no essence
to harvest upon release, prematurely preternatural,
no harvesters, either. What we laugh at is inadequacy.
For other peoples' myths, other people's legends,
to be of any use to you, you must become, a little,
those other people (penalizing acknowledgment of the exotic
is another way to reject the exotic). Though sympathy-stricken,
resist the gist of the obscurantist, blander blather,
a mutual pretense of false importance, the insult of insistence,
a disturbance in the of course, the contagion of custom,
childish admonishments against what we require of desire,
a dishonest honor, a redundancy of mind, a lack of confidence
to override conviction, inspirational delusion, the magicalcification
of reason infected with inflection, the effrontery of the upseller,
a diffident deference to those occasions when conception
doesn't lead to comprehension.

There is much we should acknowledge
but not accept.

Figure 1

Nothing happier, more sad-making,
than the children of flame-on-wind,
wet-with-dirt, racing joyously
toward the cliff.

Triumphant, pleased, pained.

The idea of *nobility* is so problematic,
sanity as a measure of vanity.

We waste more time committing exploratory
extravagances, commuting around our boundaries,
bounding around our commuted sentences,

mated, sated,
exsanguinated.

A meter down,
bones.

The Invasion

i.

wow

we mad men were right it turns out
(and the madmen were wrong)
though it's unclear how many
if any really knew it at the time and
how many just guessed
relying on cynicism and experience of men
far from the happy end of adequate
suckers & crooks
suckers & crooks

ii.

and now

everything is abandoned
but the impulse to violence
and the razing and salting is underway
and still we're chastised
for the pseudo faux pas of *I-told-you-so*
and derided for the unforgivable affront
of having sight
of being right

iii.

and now

where have all the grown-ups gone?
and why all these petulant children left behind?
here come the dead all dressed in red
unpleasant, displeasing, appeasing
a vision jest, an acquired distaste

to perceive and differentiate
to remember and dissipate
so careless of flesh
so careless of flesh

iv.

and now

the obscure and the obscene
the know-betters, the no-betters
the alcoholic, the addict chic
existing only in consensus
people are cheap
massively redundant, massively parallel
but they cost too much—
which is more important
that you do what I tell you to do
or that you not do what I tell you not to?

v.

and now

what will you do?
what do you will?
the moment that pivots into transition
can I take you seriously enough
to believe that *my* purpose, *my* mission,
is to change you?
there is so much
and so few take advantage
so many are taking advantage
but there is so little left
the one-thousand-first time can be completely different
it's only mad to believe that it will *be*
not that it can be